Tucholsky Wagner Zola Scott Sydow Freud Schlegel
Turgenev Fonatne Wallace
Twain Walther von der Vogelweide Fouqué Friedrich II. von Preußen
Weber Freiligrath Frey
Kant Ernst
Fechner Weiße Rose von Fallersleben Frommel
Fichte Richthofen
Engels Fielding Hölderlin
Fehrs Faber Flaubert Eichendorff Tacitus Dumas
Eliasberg Ebner Eschenbach
Feuerbach Maximilian I. von Habsburg Fock Zweig
Ewald Eliot Vergil
Goethe Elisabeth von Österreich London
Mendelssohn Balzac Shakespeare Dostojewski Ganghofer
Lichtenberg Rathenau Doyle Gjellerup
Trackl Stevenson Hambruch
Mommsen Tolstoi Lenz Droste-Hülshoff
Thoma Hanrieder
Dach von Arnim Hägele Hauff Humboldt
Verne
Reuter Rousseau Hagen Hauptmann Gautier
Karrillon Garschin
Defoe Baudelaire
Damaschke Hebbel
Descartes
Hegel Kussmaul Herder
Wolfram von Eschenbach Schopenhauer
Dickens Rilke George
Bronner Darwin Melville Grimm Jerome
Bebel Proust
Campe Horváth Aristoteles Federer
Bismarck Vigny Barlach Voltaire Herodot
Gengenbach Heine
Storm Casanova Tersteegen Grillparzer Georgy
Chamberlain Lessing Gilm
Langbein Gryphius
Brentano Lafontaine
Strachwitz Claudius Schiller Kralik Iffland Sokrates
Bellamy Schilling
Katharina II. von Rußland Gerstäcker Raabe Gibbon Tschechow
Löns Hesse Hoffmann Gogol Wilde Vulpius
Gleim
Luther Heym Hofmannsthal Klee Hölty Morgenstern
Roth Goedicke
Heyse Klopstock Kleist
Luxemburg Puschkin Homer
Machiavelli La Roche Horaz Mörike Musil
Navarra Aurel Musset Kierkegaard Kraft Kraus
Lamprecht Kind Hugo Moltke
Nestroy Marie de France Kirchhoff
Laotse Ipsen Liebknecht
Nietzsche Nansen Ringelnatz
Marx
von Ossietzky Lassalle Gorki Klett Leibniz
May
vom Stein Lawrence Irving
Petalozzi Knigge
Platon
Sachs Pückler Michelangelo Kafka
Poe Kock
de Sade Praetorius Liebermann
Mistral Zetkin Korolenko

The publishing house tredition has created the series **TREDITION CLASSICS**. It contains classical literature works from over two thousand years. Most of these titles have been out of print and off the bookstore shelves for decades.

The book series is intended to preserve the cultural legacy and to promote the timeless works of classical literature. As a reader of a **TREDITION CLASSICS** book, the reader supports the mission to save many of the amazing works of world literature from oblivion.

The symbol of **TREDITION CLASSICS** is Johannes Gutenberg (1400 – 1468), the inventor of movable type printing.

With the series, tredition intends to make thousands of international literature classics available in printed format again – worldwide.

All books are available at book retailers worldwide in paperback and in hardcover. For more information please visit: www.tredition.com

tredition was established in 2006 by Sandra Latusseck and Soenke Schulz. Based in Hamburg, Germany, tredition offers publishing solutions to authors and publishing houses, combined with worldwide distribution of printed and digital book content. tredition is uniquely positioned to enable authors and publishing houses to create books on their own terms and without conventional manufacturing risks.

For more information please visit: www.tredition.com

Legend Land, Vol. 1 Being a collection of some of the Old Tales told in those Western Parts of Britain served by The Great Western Railway.

George Basil Barham

Imprint

This book is part of the TREDITION CLASSICS series.

Author: George Basil Barham
Cover design: toepferschumann, Berlin (Germany)

Publisher: tredition GmbH, Hamburg (Germany)
ISBN: 978-3-8495-0463-2

www.tredition.com
www.tredition.de

Copyright:
The content of this book is sourced from the public domain.

The intention of the TREDITION CLASSICS series is to make world literature in the public domain available in printed format. Literary enthusiasts and organizations worldwide have scanned and digitally edited the original texts. tredition has subsequently formatted and redesigned the content into a modern reading layout. Therefore, we cannot guarantee the exact reproduction of the original format of a particular historic edition. Please also note that no modifications have been made to the spelling, therefore it may differ from the orthography used today.

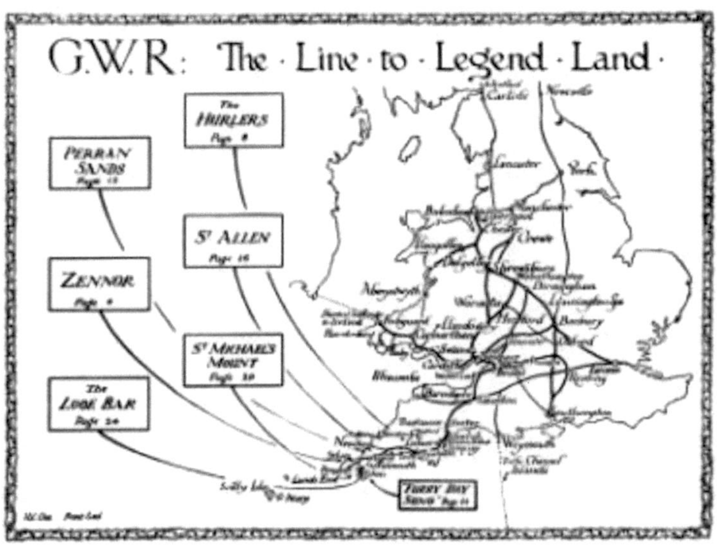

G.W.R : The · Line · to · Legend · Land ·
The HURLERS Page
PERRAN SANDS Page
ZENNOR Page
The LOOE BAR Page
St ALLEN Page
St MICHAELS MOUNT Page
TORREY BAY Page
Scilly Isles
Land's End

LEGEND LAND

**Being a collection of some of the
OLD TALES told in those Western
Parts of Britain served by the
GREAT WESTERN RAILWAY, now
retold by *LYONESSE***

VOLUME ONE

CONTENTS AND ILLUSTRATIONS

This is a reprint in book form of the first series of *The Line to Legend Land* leaflets, together with a Supplement, "The Furry Day Song."

The Map at the beginning provides a guide to the localities of the six Cornish legends and the "Furry Day Song"; that at the back to the six stories of Wales.

Printed by Spottiswoode, Ballantyne & Company Limited,
One New Street Square, London, E.C.4

[3]

FOREWORD

In those older, simpler days, when reading was a rare accomplishment, our many times great-grandparents would gather round the blazing fire of kitchen or hall on the long, dark winter nights and pass away the hours before bedtime in conversation and story-telling.

The old stories were told again and again. The children learned them in their earliest years and passed them on to their children and grandchildren in turn. And, as is natural, in all this telling the stories changed little by little. New and more familiar characters were introduced, or a story-teller with more vivid imagination than his fellows would add a bit here and there to make a better tale of it.

But in origin most of these old legends date from the very dawn of our history. In a primitive form they were probably told round the camp-fires of that British army that went out to face invading Cæsar.

Then with the spread of education they began to die. When many folk could read and books grew cheap there was no longer the need to call upon memory for the old-fashioned romances.

Yet there have always been those who loved the old tales best, and they wrote them down before it was too late, so that they might be preserved for ever. A few of them are retold briefly here.

All people should like the old stories; all nice people do. To them I commend these tales of Legend Land, in the hope that they may grow to love them and the countries about which they are written.

LYONESSE

[4]

THE MERMAID OF ZENNOR

[5]

C arved on one of the pews in the church of Zennor in West Cornwall is a strange figure of a mermaid. Depicted with flowing hair, a mirror in one hand and a comb in the other, the Zennor folk tell a strange story about her.

Years and years ago, they say, a beautiful and richly dressed lady used to attend the church sometimes. Nobody knew where she came from, although her unusual beauty and her glorious voice caused her to be the subject of discussion throughout the parish.

So attractive was she that half the young men of the village fell in love with her, and one of them, Mathey Trewella, a handsome youth and one of the best singers in the neighbourhood, determined that he would discover who she was.

The beautiful stranger had smiled at him in church one Sunday, and after service he followed her as she walked away towards the cliffs.

Mathey Trewella never returned to Zennor, nor did the lovely stranger ever attend church again.

Years passed by, and Mathey's strange disappearance was almost forgotten when, one Sunday morning, a ship cast anchor off Pendower Cove, near Zennor. The captain of the vessel was sitting idling on the deck when he heard a beautiful voice hailing him from the sea. Looking over the side he saw the mermaid, her long yellow hair floating all around her.

She asked him to be so kind as to pull up his anchor, for it was resting upon the doorway of her house [6] under the sea and she was anxious to get back to Mathey, her husband, and her children.

In alarm, the captain weighed anchor and stood out to sea, for sailors fear that mermaids will bring bad luck. But later he returned and told the Zennor folk of Mathey's fate, and they, to commemorate the strange event, and to warn other young men against the wiles of the merrymaids, had the mermaid figure carved in the church.

And there it is to-day for all the world to see, and to prove, to those who do not believe the old stories, the truth of poor Mathey Trewella's sad fate.

Zennor is a lovely moorland village in the neighbourhood of some of the wildest scenery in Cornwall. To the south-west rugged moors stretch away to the Land's End. To the north a quarter of an hour's walk brings you to the coast with its sheltered coves and its cruel cliffs. Gurnard's Head, one of the most famous of all Cornish promontories, is less than two miles away. Grim, remote, yet indescribably fascinating, the country around Zennor is typical of that far western corner of England which is swept continually by the great health-giving winds of the Atlantic.

In its sheltered valleys flowers bloom all the year round. On its bold hill-tops, boulder-strewn and wild, there remain still the old mysterious stones and the queer beehive huts erected by men who inhabited this land in the dark days before Christianity.

Gorse and heather riot over the moorland. There [7] is a charm and peace about this too little known country that compels health and well-being.

Yet Zennor is only five and a half miles by the moorland road from St. Ives, that picturesque little fishing town that artists and golfers know so well. St. Ives, less than seven hours' journey from Paddington, is an ideal centre from which to explore the coast and moorland beauties of England's furthest west.

The Mermaid of Zennor: Bench End in Zennor Church

[8]

THE STONE MEN OF ST. CLEER

[9]

A thousand feet above sea level among the heather and bracken of Craddock Moor, four or five miles north of Liskeard, you may find to-day the remains of three ancient stone circles known as "The Hurlers." Antiquaries will tell you that the Druids first erected them, but the people of the countryside know better. From father to son, from grandparent to child, through long centuries, the story has been handed down of how "The Hurlers" came to be fixed in eternal stillness high up there above the little village of St. Cleer.

Exactly how long ago it was nobody knows, but it happened in those early days when pious saints were settling down in the remote parts of savage Cornwall and striving to convert the wild Cornish from their pagan ways.

Then, as even to this day, the game of Hurling—a sort of primitive Rugby football—was a popular pastime with the people. Village used to play against village, with goals perhaps four or five miles apart. And the good folk of St. Cleer were as fond of the game as any of their neighbours—so fond, in fact, that they would play it on any and every occasion, despite the admonitions of their local saint and parson, after whom the village was named.

Again and again he would notice that his little church was empty on Sunday mornings while the shouts and noise of a hard-fought Hurling match drifted across the moorland in through the open church door. Again and again he would take his flock [10] to task for their godless ways and their Sabbath-breaking games. But it was of little use. For a Sunday or two they would be penitent and attend service. Then would come a fine morning, and a challenge perhaps from the Hurlers of St. Ive or North Hill, on the other side of the moors, and the young men would decide to chance another lecture from the patient saint, and out they would go to the hillside to do battle for the honour of their parish.

But even the patience of saints comes to an end at last, and good St. Cleer saw something more than words was needed to lead his people into the right way. And so it happened one Sunday morning, in the midst of a hot tussle on Craddock Moor, the outraged St. Cleer arrived in search of his erring flock.

He bade them cease their game at once and return to church. Some of them obeyed, wandering sheepishly off down the hill; some were defiant and told the worthy man to go back to his prayers and not to come up there to spoil sport.

Then St. Cleer spoke in anger. Raising his staff he told them in solemn and awful tones that it should be as they had chosen. Since they preferred their game on the moor to their service in church, on the moor at their game they should stay for ever. He lowered his staff and to the horror of all onlookers the defiant ones were seen to be turned into stone.

Many centuries have passed since then. Time, wind and rain have weathered the stone men out of all semblance of humanity. Some have been destroyed, but most still remain as an awful example [11] to impious Sabbath profaners. And there you may see them silent and still, just as they were struck on that grim Sunday in the dark long ago.

The glorious moorland, rugged and wild, stretches all about them—a wonderful walking country, where one may escape from all cares and wander for hours amid the bracken and sweet-smelling grasses and find strange prehistoric remains seldom visited by any but the moorland sheep and the wild birds. It is a country of vast spaces and far views. You may see on one hand the Severn Sea, on the other the Channel; to the east the upstanding blue hills of Dartmoor and to the west the rugged highlands by Land's End—and then trudge back at night weary but happy to Liskeard, described as "the pleasantest town in Cornwall," and find it hard to believe that only five hours away is the toil and turmoil of London.

"The Hurlers," St. Cleer

[12]

HOW ST. PIRAN CAME TO CORNWALL

S ome sixteen hundred years ago, so tradition tells, there lived in the South of Ireland a very holy man named Piran. Such was his piety that he was able to perform miracles. Once he fed ten Irish kings and their armies for ten days on end with three cows. Men sorely wounded in battle were brought to him to be cured, and he cured them. Yet the Irish grew jealous of his power and decided he must be killed.

And so one stormy, boisterous morning the pious [13] Piran was brought in chains to the summit of a high cliff, and with a huge millstone tied to his neck his ungrateful neighbours hurled him into the raging billows beneath. This horrible deed was marked, as the holy man left the top of the cliff, with a blinding flash of lightning and a terrifying crash of thunder, and then, to the amazement of the savages who had thus sought to destroy him, a wonderful thing happened.

As man and millstone reached the sea the storm instantly ceased. The sun shone out, the waves and the wind died down, and, peering over the edge of the cliff, the wondering crowd saw the holy man, seated peacefully upon a floating millstone, drifting slowly away in the direction of the Cornish shore, some hundreds of miles to the south-east.

St. Piran's millstone bore him safely across the Atlantic waves until at length—on the fifth day of March—it grounded gently upon the Cornish coast, between Newquay and Perranporth, on that glorious stretch of sand known to-day as Perran Beach. Here the Saint landed, and, taking his millstone with him, proceeded a little distance inland and set himself to work to convert the heathen Cornish to Christianity.

He built himself a little chapel in the sands and lived a useful and pious life for many years, loved by his people, until at last, at the great age of two hundred and six, he died. Then his sorrowing flock buried him and built over his grave St. Piran's Chapel, the remains of which you can see to-day hidden away in the sandhills of the Penhale Sands.

[14]

Although Cornwall can boast many saints, St. Piran has greater right than any other to be called the patron of the Duchy. To him the Cornish in the old days attributed a vast number of good actions, among them the discovery of tin, the mining of which has for centuries formed one of the chief Cornish industries.

This came about, according to the old story, from the saint making use of some strange black stones that he found, to make a foundation for his fire. The heat being more intense than usual one day, these stones melted and a stream of white metal flowed from them.

The saint and his companion, St. Chiwidden, told the Cornish people of their discovery, and taught them to dig and smelt the ore, thus bringing much prosperity to the country, the story of which eventually reached the far-away Ph[oe]nicians and brought them in their ships to trade with the Cornish for their valuable metal.

Good St. Piran has left his name all over the wonderful country south-west of Newquay. In Perranporth, with its rocks and caves and glorious bathing beach; in St. Piran's Round, that strange old earth-work not far away; in the parish of Perranzabuloe, which means Perran in the Sands; in Perranwell, near Falmouth, and even further south in Perranuthnoe, which looks out across the waters of Mounts Bay.

But although memorials of him are to be found over most of South Cornwall, it is the district of the [15] Perran Sands, where he landed, lived and died, that is his true home. There, where the soft Atlantic breezes or the fierce winter gales sweep in to Perran Bay, you may look out over the dancing sea towards Ireland and America with nothing but Atlantic rollers between, or wander amid the waste of sand dunes that comprise the Perran Sands and breathe in health with every breath you take.

Perranporth is on the edge of these sandhills, which stretch away north-east to within four miles of Newquay—all within seven hours' journey from London.

St. Piran's Chapel

[16]

THE LOST CHILD OF ST. ALLEN

They never talk of fairies in Cornwall; what "foreigners" call fairies the Cornish call "piskies," or "small people." And all about the Duchy piskies still abound for those who are fitted to see them. The old folk will still tell you many strange stories of the piskies. One of the best known is that of the lost child of St. Allen. St. Allen is a parish on the high ground about four miles from Truro, and there, in the little hamlet of Treonike, or, as it is now called, Trefronick, on a [17] lovely spring evening years and years ago, a small village boy wandered out to pick flowers in a little copse not far from his parents' cottage.

His mother, looking from the kitchen door, saw him happily engaged in his innocent amusement, then turned to make ready the supper for her good man, whom she saw trudging home in the distance across the fields. When, a few minutes later, she went to call her boy in to his evening meal, he had vanished.

At first it was thought that the child had merely wandered further into the wood, but after a while, when he did not return, his parents grew alarmed and went in search of him. Yet no sign of the boy was discovered.

For two days the villagers sought high and low for the missing child, and then, on the morning of the third day, to the delight of the distracted parents, their boy was found sleeping peacefully upon a bed of fern within a few yards of the place where his mother had last seen him. He was perfectly well, quite happy, and entirely ignorant of the length of time that had elapsed. And he had a wonderful story to tell.

While picking the flowers, he said, he had heard a bird singing in more beautiful tones than any he had heard before. Going into the wood to see what strange songster this was, the sound changed to most wonderful music which compelled him to follow it. Thus lured onward he came at length to the edge of an enchanted lake, and he noticed that night had fallen but that the sky was ablaze with huge stars. [18] Then more stars rose up all around him, and, looking, he saw that each was in reality a pisky. These small people formed themselves into a procession, singing strange fascinating songs the while, and under the leadership of one who was more brilliant and more beautiful than the rest they led the boy through their dwelling place. This, he said, was like a palace. Crystal pillars supported arches hung with jewels which glistened with every colour of the rainbow. Far more wonderful, the child said, were the crystals than any he had seen in a Cornish mine.

The piskies were very kind to him, and seemed to enjoy his wonder and astonishment at their gorgeous cave. They gave him a fairy meal of the purest honey spread on dainty little cakes, and when at last he grew tired numbers of the small folk fell to work to build him a bed of fern. Then, crowding around him, they sang him to sleep with a strange soothing lullaby, which for the rest of his life he was always just on the point of remembering, but which as certainly escaped him. He remembered nothing more until he was awakened and taken home to his parents.

The wise folk of St. Allen maintained that only a child of the finest character ever received such honour from the small people, and that the fact that they had shown him the secrets of their hidden dwelling augured that for ever afterwards they would keep him under their especial care. And so it was; the boy lived to a ripe old age and prospered amazingly. He never knew illness or misfortune, and died at last in his sleep; and those that were near him say that as [19] he breathed his last a strange music filled the room. Some say that the piskies still haunt the woods and fields around Trefronick, but that they only show themselves to children and grown-ups of simple, trusting nature. Anyhow, those that wish to try to see them may reach the place where the lost child was spirited away in an hour and a half's walk from Truro, Cornwall's cathedral city, which is at the head of one of the most beautiful rivers in the world.

The trip from Truro down the Truro river and the Fal to Falmouth at any time of the year is a pleasurable experience that can never be forgotten. Truro is an ideal centre for South Cornwall. Wild sea coast and moorland, and woods and sheltered creeks, are all close at hand, yet the city itself has the cloistered calm peculiar to all our cathedral towns.

The tourist neglects Truro too much, for as a lover of the Duchy once said: "It is the most convenient town in Cornwall; it seems to be within an hour and a half's journey of any part of the county."

Truro Cathedral

[20]

THE GIANTS WHO BUILT THE MOUNT

S t. Michael's Mount, that impressive castle-crowned pyramid of rock that rises from the waters of Mounts Bay, was not always an island. In fact, it is not always an island now. At low tide you may reach it from the mainland along a causeway. But once upon a time the Mount stood in the midst of a forest; its old name, "Caraclowse in Cowse," means "the Grey Rock in the Wood," and that was at the time when the Giants built it.

[21]

Cormoran was one of the Giants; he lived in this great western forest, which is now swallowed up by the sea, and there he determined to erect for himself a stronghold that should rise well above the trees. So he set to work to collect huge stones from the neighbouring granite hills, and his new home grew apace.

But the labour of searching far afield for suitable stones, and of carrying them to the forest and piling them one upon another, was a wearying task even for a giant, and as Cormoran grew tired he forced his unfortunate Giantess wife, Cormelian, to help him in his task, and to her he gave the most toilsome of the labour.

Was there a gigantic boulder in a far part of the Duchy that Cormoran coveted, unhappy Cormelian was sent to fetch it; and she, like a dutiful wife, never complained, but went meekly about her work, collecting the finest and biggest stones and carrying them back to the forest in her apron. Meanwhile Cormoran, growing more lazy, spent much of his time in sleep, waking up only very occasionally to admonish his wife or to incite her to greater efforts.

One day, when Cormelian had been twice as far as the Bodmin moors to fetch some particularly fine stones Cormoran had seen, and was about to set off on a third journey, she, noticing her husband fast asleep, thought to save herself another weary walk by going only a short distance and breaking off some huge masses of greenstone rock which existed in the neighbourhood and placing them upon the nearly [22] completed Mount without being seen.

Although Cormoran had insisted that the stone be grey, Cormelian could see no reason why one stone was not as good as another.

So, carrying out her plan, she was returning with the first enormous piece of greenstone, walking ever so carefully so as not to awaken Cormoran, when, unfortunately, he did awake. He flew into a terrible rage on seeing how his wife was trying to delude him, and, rising with a dreadful threat, he ran after her, overtaking her just before she reached the Mount.

Scolding her for her deceit, he gave her a terrific box on the ear. Poor Cormelian, in her fright, dropped the huge greenstone she was carrying, and ran sobbing from her angry husband to seek refuge in the deepest part of the forest; and it was not until Cormoran himself had finished building the Mount that she would return to him.

And to-day, as you walk along the causeway from Marazion to St. Michael's Mount, you will see on your right hand an isolated mass of greenstone, the very rock that Cormelian dropped. It is called Chapel Rock now, because years and years afterwards, when pious monks lived upon the summit of the Mount and devout pilgrims used to visit their church to pay homage at a shrine, they built a little chapel, upon poor Cormelian's green rock, of which only a few stones now remain.

You may visit Chapel Rock and St. Michael's Mount from Penzance, which is between three and [23] four miles away and is the ideal centre for some of the most wonderful scenery in Cornwall. Both Land's End and the Lizard are within easy reach of this, England's westernmost town, where a climate that rivals that of the Mediterranean may be enjoyed in the depth of winter. Semi-tropical flowers and trees bloom in the open, and in February and early March — in what is, in fact, winter weather for those in less favoured parts — Penzance and its neighbourhood are surrounded by glorious spring flowers, the growing of which forms a very considerable industry.

London and our other big towns often get their first glimpse of coming spring in the narcissi and wallflowers grown around the shores of Mounts Bay, and packed off to the grim cold cities only a few hours away.

St. Michael's Mount

[24]

Cooper

THE TASKS OF TREGEAGLE

T he name of the demon Tregeagle is a household word in nearly every part of Cornwall. His wild spirit rages of nights along the rocky coasts, across the bleak moors and through the sheltered valleys. For Tregeagle is a Cornish "Wandering Jew"; his spirit can never rest, since in life he was the most evil man the Duchy ever knew.

His story, as the legend has it, is that he was a man who amassed great wealth by robbing his neighbours [25] in the cruellest manner. As he approached the end of his most evil life remorse seized him. There was no sin he had not committed, and hoping to escape from the just reward of so wicked a life, in the hereafter, he lavished money upon the Church and the poor, trusting to obtain the help of the holy priests to save him from the clutches of the Evil One.

The priests, ever anxious to save a soul, banded themselves together, and by constant prayer and powerful exorcisms kept the powers of darkness at bay, and Tregeagle died and was buried in St. Breock Church. But the demons were not so ready to give up what they felt was their lawful prey. An important lawsuit occurred shortly after his death, and as the judge was about to give his decision against the unjustly accused defendant, to the horror of all in court, the gaunt figure of the dead Tregeagle stalked into the room. His evidence saved the defendant.

Now Tregeagle being brought from the grave, despite the honesty of his mission, placed himself once more in danger of the demons. The defendant, who had raised the spirit, calmly left him to the Churchmen to put once more to rest, and after a long conference, presided over by the Prior of Bodmin, it was decided that the only hope of ultimate peace for the evil man's spirit was that he be set to some task which might last until the Day of Judgment. And so long as he worked unceasingly at that task he might still hope for salvation.

So the task appointed him was to empty out [26] Dozmary Pool, a gloomy lake on the Bodmin Moors, with a limpet-shell with a hole in it. For years Tregeagle laboured at this, until one day during a terrible storm he ceased work for a moment. Then the demons descended upon him. He fled from his pursuers, and only escaped them by leaping right across the lake—for demons cannot cross water—and rushing for sanctuary to the little chapel on the Roche Rock, where he managed just in time to get his head in at the east window. But the howls of the demons outside, and the roaring of the terrified Tregeagle within, made the life of the unfortunate priest of the Roche chapel unbearable, and he appealed to his brethren of the Church to do something about it. So they bound the wicked spirit with holy spells and took him safely across to the north coast, where another task was set him. He was to weave a truss of sand and spin a sand rope to bind it with. But as soon as he started on his work the winds or the waves destroyed it, and the luckless creature's roars of anger so disturbed the countryside that the holy St. Petroc was prevailed upon to move him once more, to a wilder part of the country, and the saint took him to the coast near Helston.

Here Tregeagle was set to the task of carrying all the sand from the beach below Bareppa across the estuary of the Looe river to Porthleven, for St. Petroc knew that each tide would sweep the sand back again and the task could never be completed. But the demons were always watching Tregeagle, and one of them contrived one day to trip him up as he was [27] wading across the river. The sand poured from the huge sack Tregeagle was carrying and dammed up the stream, thus forming the Looe Pool, which you may see to-day just by Helston, and the Looe Bar, which separates it from the sea.

Tregeagle's next task he is engaged upon to-day. He was taken to near the Land's End, and there he is still endeavouring to sweep the sand from Porthcurnow Cove round the headland of Tol-Peden-Penwith into Nanjisal Bay, and on many a winter night if you are there you can hear him howling and roaring at the hopelessness of his task.

These scenes of Tregeagle's labours are all situated amid most glorious scenery. Dozmary Pool, bleak and lonely amid the Bodmin Moors, the little chapel on the Roche Rock near St. Austell, and the beautiful Looe Pool by Helston, that attractive little town on a hillside, which is the tourist centre for that country full of colour, deep sheltered valleys, and magnificent coast scenery, the Lizard peninsula.

Porthcurnow, the miserable man's present abode, you will find nestling amid the grim cliffs near the Land's End. And if you doubt this sad history of the demon-ridden Tregeagle, go and look at the Looe Bar and explain if you can how otherwise so strange a place could have been created.

The Roche Rocks

[28]

THE LADY OF LLYN-Y-FAN FACH

[29]

Not many miles from Llandovery, in the midst of glorious mountain scenery, is a lovely little lake known as Llyn-y-Fan-Fach, the scene of a very remarkable occurrence. Once upon a time a simple cowherd, eating his frugal meal by the edge of the water, observed with amazement, seated upon the calm surface of the lake, the most beautiful woman he had ever seen. So great was his admiration for her that he cried out, and she, turning to him, gave a rapturous smile and silently disappeared beneath the waters.

The peasant was distracted, for he had fallen deeply in love with the beautiful lady. He waited until dark, but she did not appear again; but at daybreak the next morning he returned once more, and was again rewarded by the sight of his enchantress and another of her alluring smiles.

Several times more he saw her and each time he besought her to be his wife, but she only smiled and disappeared, until at length one evening, just as the sun was setting, the beautiful lady appeared, and this time, instead of diving beneath the surface, she came to the shore, and, after some persuasion, consented to marry the youth. But she made one condition: if ever he should strike her three blows without cause she would leave him, she said, and their marriage would be at an end.

So the two were married happily and went to live at Esgair Laethdy, near Myddfai, the maiden bringing with her as dowry a large number of cattle and horses which she called up from the bottom of the lake.

[30]

For years the couple lived in great prosperity and happiness, and three handsome sons were born to them; then the day arrived when husband and wife were setting out for a christening, and, being rather late, the husband slapped his wife merrily on the shoulder, urging her to hurry. Sadly she reminded him that he had struck her the first of the causeless blows.

Years passed by, and the couple were at a wedding. In the midst of all the merry-making the wife burst suddenly into tears. Patting her sympathetically on the arm, the man inquired the cause of her weeping, and she, sobbing the harder, reminded him that he had struck her a second time.

Now that he had only one chance left, the husband was particularly careful never to forget and strike the third and last blow; but, after a long while, at a funeral one day, while all were sobbing and weeping, the beautiful lady suddenly began laughing merrily. Touching her gently to quiet her, the husband realised that the end had come.

"The last blow has been struck; our marriage is ended," said the wife, now in tears; and with that she started off across the hills to their farm. There she called together her cattle and other stock, which immediately obeyed her voice, and, led by the beautiful lady, the whole procession moved off across the mountains back to the lake.

Among the animals was a team of four oxen which were ploughing at the time. They followed, too, plough and all, and, they say, to this very day you may [31] see a well-marked furrow running right across the Myddfai mountain to the edge of Llyn-y-Fan-Fach, which proves the truth of this story.

The disconsolate husband never saw his lady again, but she used sometimes to appear to her sons, and she gave them such wonderful knowledge that all three became the most famous doctors in that part of Wales.

Llandovery, from which place you may visit the scenes of this legend, is a charming little town in East Carmarthenshire, situated in glorious surroundings of mountains, vale, and moorland, where some of the finest salmon and trout fishing in South Wales may be enjoyed. It stands in the beautiful Towy Valley, on a branch line which runs up into the mountain country from Llanelly. Llandovery is famous for its air, which is said to be the purest and most bracing in the district.

Landovery Castle

[32]

ST. DAVID AND HIS MOTHER

[33]

St. David, everybody knows, is the patron saint of Wales, but few know the unique little "village-city," the smallest cathedral city in the United Kingdom, St. Davids, in the far south-west of Wales; and fewer still the story of the holy David himself. This story really begins with St. Patrick, the patron saint of Ireland. As the old legends tell, St. Patrick sailed on his mission to Ireland from the neighbourhood of present-day St. Davids, and he liked the look of the country so well that many years afterwards he established there a sort of missionary college known as "Ty Gwyn," or the "White House," and here on the slopes of Carn Llidi some of the earliest of the old Celtic holy men and women were educated.

Among them, some fifteen hundred years ago, was a Welsh Princess named Non, daughter of Cynyr of Caer Gawch, a powerful chieftain of the district. Non was as pious as she was beautiful. There were few maidens in the land who could compare with her.

But on what seemed to be an evil day—although it became really for Wales a very lucky one—a barbarous chieftain from the north, called Sant son of Ceredig, espied the rapturous Non picking flowers on a lonely part of the hillside, and in the manner of those boisterous times he decided to carry her off and make her his wife. And so despite her struggles the unfortunate Non was kidnapped.

After some while she managed to escape from her fierce captor and returned to live in a little cottage on the cliffs just south of St. Davids, where subsequently [34] a son was born to her. At the time of his birth they say Non clutched at a stone in the wall of her cottage room, and the marks of her fingers remained on it for ever. This stone was seen by many people for years afterwards and was eventually placed over her tomb.

The little son grew up and was baptised David by a kinsman of Non's, one St. Ailbe. Like his mother, he was sent to the "Ty Gwyn" to school and he became a very pious youth. Then he was sent away to the holy St. Illtyd to be trained as a priest.

His grandfather Cynyr, who was by no means a holy man, growing remorseful in his old age, was so much impressed by David's piety, that for the good of his soul he made over to him all his lands, and on this estate David founded a sanctuary for men of all tribes and nationalities, and, to mark the privileged ground, he caused a deep trench to be dug, and traces of this trench you may find to-day known as "The Monk's Dyke."

Here in his sanctuary the holy David lived his pious, peaceful life for many years, converting the heathen and performing miracles. And when at last he died his sorrowing companions built over his grave a great church to his memory, which years afterwards, when David had become recognised as a saint, was replaced by the wonderful old building which stands there now — St. David's Cathedral.

The remains of Non's old cottage on the cliff, which the monks afterwards turned into a Chapel, may still be seen, and because of her holy life she [35] also became a saint. Near to the ruined Chapel you will find, too, St. Non's well, or St. Nunn's well as it is sometimes called, from which the holy woman drew her water when she lived her lonely life at the time of St. David's birth.

Quaint little St. Davids lies far from a railway station, but a road motor service will take you there in a two hours' journey across magnificent country from Haverfordwest in Pembrokeshire, or you may approach it along a wild, hilly road from Fishguard.

St. Davids is unique: it is literally both village and city. Situated right by the coast of picturesque St. Bride's Bay on one side and Whitesand Bay on the other, it occupies a position of peculiar beauty. Good bathing, fishing and shooting abound; there is a golf course, and, chief of its attractions, the glorious Norman architecture of its jewel-like cathedral, its ancient monastic ruins, its old cross and all the other relics of the careful work of the old ecclesiastical builders in the far-away days.

St. David's Cathedral

[36]

THE VENGEANCE OF THE FAIRIES

[37]

Overlooking the sea that washes the beautiful coast of the Gower Peninsula in Glamorganshire stands the ruined castle of Pennard. All about it is a waste of sandhills, beneath which, so the old stories have it, a considerable village lies buried. For it is told that in the old days, when the lands about Pennard were fertile and populous, the lord of the castle was holding a great feast one day to rejoice over the wedding of his daughter.

This happy event was being celebrated by the villagers too, and, unknown to lord or serf, by the "Tylwyth Teg," or the fairy folk who abounded in the neighbourhood, for the little people enjoy an innocent merry-making as much as do mere mortals.

And that night, long after the villagers had gone to bed, the festivities in the castle were continued. Wine flowed free and the revellers became more and more boisterous. From mere jesting they came to quarrelling, and, in the midst of their drunken orgy, there was heard an alarm. A sentry on the walls of the castle reported that he heard stealthy movements in the distance as of a large number of people approaching with care.

The frenzied warriors, fearing a surprise from their enemies, armed themselves and rushed from the castle to attack the intruders. They, too, could hear a gentle murmur in the valley below, and towards it they charged, uttering terrible threats, striking right and left with their swords at the unseen foe. But, apart from a few shadowy forms that quickly faded [38] away into the undergrowth, nothing was to be seen, and at length the knights and soldiers returned rather crestfallen, and much more sober, to their stronghold.

Now the truth of the whole matter was that the alarm had been caused by the festivities of the fairies, and they were so deeply incensed at having their party broken up by this violent intrusion of wine-maddened men that they determined to be revenged.

That very night the whole family set out for Ireland, where they descended upon a huge mountain of sand, and each one of the small people, loading himself with as much sand as he could carry, returned to Pennard and deposited it upon the village at the base of the castle, intending to bury both village and castle in sand.

To and fro the fairies went, intent upon their task of vengeance, and, when morning broke, those in the castle looked out to see what they thought was a violent sand-storm raging. By mid-day the village below the castle was overwhelmed, and those in the stronghold began to fear that it too would be smothered. But fortunately for them the Irish sand-mountain gave out, and the fairies' complete vengeance was thwarted. Still, they had destroyed the rich and valuable lands that belonged to the castle, and from that day its fortunes and those of its lords began to decline.

In proof of this story the old Irish records maintain that an extraordinary storm arose that night and blew away a whole sand-mountain.

[39]

Few tourists ever explore the beauties of the little Gower Peninsula, save holiday-makers from the neighbouring town of Swansea; yet it is a country of amazing charm, with a glorious coast and high ridges of heather and moorland. It is only about eighty square miles in extent, but it has over fifty miles of coast.

Remote from the world, this country, with its churches, castles, and many prehistoric remains, is an ideal holiday land.

Pennard Castle

[40]

THE OLD WOMAN WHO FOOLED THE DEVIL

[41]

O ne of the most beautiful spots in all Wales is the Devil's Bridge—an easy excursion into the hills from Aberystwyth—which spans the gorge through which the Mynach cataract descends in four boiling leaps a distance of two hundred and ten feet. How this place received its name is an old story, which goes back to the days before the monks of sweetly named Strata Florida, who subsequently replaced the earlier bridge across the gorge.

The beginning of the story is told in an old rhyme which runs:—

"Old Megan Llandunach of Pont-y-Mynach

Had lost her only cow;

Across the ravine the cow was seen,

But to get it she could not tell how."

Such was the sad plight of old Megan, who was bemoaning the loss of her property on the wrong side of the gorge so many years ago, when there appeared to her suddenly a cowled monk, whose dark face was scarcely discernible, with a rosary hanging to his girdle, and a deep but pleasant voice.

Enquiring the cause of her distress, the monk, in sympathetic tones, promised to aid her. He would, he said, build a bridge across the ravine, so that she might recover her lost cow, if she would promise to give him the first living being to cross the bridge.

This seemed a natural enough suggestion to the sorrowing old dame, for the good monks of the neighbourhood were ever about the countryside, [42] seeking converts; so Megan agreed, and the monk set to work with amazing energy and skill to construct the bridge. And as he worked Megan sat on a boulder and watched him.

Before sundown the marvellous bridge was finished, and the smiling monk, walking over it, invited Megan to follow him and seek her cow. But Megan had been observant. She had noticed two or three things. One, that there was no cross attached to the monk's rosary; another, that while he was labouring at his building he had slipped, and his left leg was exposed through his long habit, and the knee was on the back of the leg, and not the front; also the leg ended not in a foot, but in a cloven hoof.

And cunning old Megan was taking no chances. Feeling in the pocket of her skirt she found a crust, and walking to her side of the bridge she called to a black cur that was playing about. Hurling the crust across the bridge she bade the dog fetch it. He ran over the bridge, and Megan, smiling at the monk, thanked him, and told him to take the dog as his reward.

The devil, realising that he had been fooled, disappeared in an awe-inspiring cloud of smoke and sulphur fumes; but the bridge remained, and its name to this day recalls the discomfiture of his evil plans. So, having fooled the devil, Megan was able to recover her lost cow.

Wordsworth and Borrow, among other famous writers, have immortalised the impressive beauties of the Devil's Bridge and its roaring cataract. It is [43] easily reached from that most attractive of Welsh seaside towns, Aberystwyth, and lies in a country dominated by great Plinlimmon, from the top of which a view of unrivalled beauty may be obtained.

All about this country of mountain and moorland are scenes of intense historic interest and natural beauty. It is a district bleak and bracing on the summits, warm and sheltered in the valleys, and as yet quite unspoiled by the crowd, as too is the charming town which is the centre of this country.

Aberystwyth retains the quiet charm of an old-world "watering-place," and glories in its wonderful climate and healing sea breezes that blow in across Cardigan Bay, which have won for it its reputation in winter and summer for being a British Biarritz.

Devil's Bridge, Aberystwyth

[44]

THE WOMEN SOLDIERS OF FISHGUARD

[45]

They tell a story down in Pembrokeshire of how the Welsh country-women once defeated an invading army. It was in the days of the Napoleonic wars when, on a winter's afternoon, four hostile ships appeared unexpectedly off Fishguard Bay. On board were fourteen hundred soldiers intent upon an invasion of Britain.

The wild country of the far west of Wales was in those days even more remote than it is now. In the neighbourhood were but three hundred militiamen, and the invaders had an easy task in landing at Llanwnda, about two miles away from modern Fishguard, in a charming sheltered inlet known as Careg Gwastad Bay.

But the gallant Welsh determined to drive out the invader. They were furious, and, armed with scythes and other farm implements, they quickly gathered together. For such firearms as they had there was little ammunition, so they stripped the roof of beautiful little St. David's Cathedral of its lead in order to make bullets.

And the women of the country followed their men. Clad in their red cloaks and high black steeple-crowned hats, in the distance they had all the appearance of regular soldiers, and the leader of the defending forces was quick to realise this fact.

He marshalled them into something like military formation and marched them about in various places where they could be seen by the invading troops. Up and down hill the willing Welsh women trudged until darkness fell and they were tired out.

[46]

Meanwhile there was consternation in the invaders' camp. The commander knew that scarlet was the colour of our soldiers' uniform, and he could only conclude that overwhelming reinforcements were arriving from the interior. Believing his cause hopeless, he sent in a letter under a flag of truce to the British commander, offering to surrender, and within three days of landing the whole invading force was made prisoner.

There is an amazing sequel to this invasion, for it seems that most of the troops employed were criminals, released from French gaols, and other similar undesirable characters, and since they had failed in their primary object the French Government was none too anxious to have them back in France again, and refused to exchange them.

The British Government was no more pleased than the French to have so unsavoury a band of ruffians in its midst, and it had at last to force the Frenchmen to receive their own rogues back again. This was done by threatening that if the prisoners were not exchanged within a certain time they would be landed with arms on the coast of Brittany and left to do their worst.

The French preferred to have them in control and exchanges were promptly arranged, the discomfited invaders going back, it is assumed, to the safety of the French prisons from which they had been brought.

Careg Gwastad Bay, the scene of this landing, is but one of the many fascinating little inlets that [47] abound along the coast in the Fishguard neighbourhood. Excellent fishing—for sea fish, trout, sewin, and often salmon—abounds off the coast or in the streams. Fishguard is fortunate in possessing a modern steam-heated hotel close to the station—the Fishguard Bay—which is equipped with every modern luxury and comfort.

From Fishguard one can approach, too, that romantic and historic country known as Kemaes Land, which extends away to the borders of Cardiganshire, a country—bounded on the north by the cliffs that run down to the waters of Cardigan Bay—full of old churches, castles, and strange remains of earlier civilisations, standing remote upon its mountains and moorlands.

This is a land of flowers too, for its mild winter climate enables many plants to flourish in the open that must seek the security of greenhouses in the bleaker parts of the south.

Welsh National Costume

[48]

HOW BALA LAKE BEGAN

[49]

T here is a Welsh couplet, still well known in the neighbourhood of beautiful Bala Lake in Merionethshire, which, translated into English, runs:

> *"Bala old the lake has had, and Bala new*
>
> *The lake will have, and Llanfor, too."*

For there is an ages-old belief in the countryside that Bala will continue to grow bigger until it has swallowed up the village of Llanfor, now about a couple of miles from the water's edge.

According to the old story the site of the original town is near the middle of the present lake, at a spot opposite Llangower. There, years and years ago, a peaceful community lived a happy, prosperous life in their houses clustering around a well called Ffynnon Gwyer, or Gower's Well.

Only one very important thing had these long-ago people to remember, and that was to cover up their well every night, otherwise, as they knew from their fathers and grandfathers before them, the spirit of the well would grow angry with them and wreak some dire punishment upon them.

But one night, after some special festivities, the guardian of the well forgot his task. Too late this omission was discovered, for as soon as the last inhabitant was in bed, the well began to gush forth water.

Soon the whole village was in a state of alarm. The quickly rising waters began to flow into the cottages, and young and old rushed to Ffynnon [50] Gower, which they realised was the cause of their distress. There they saw a great stream of water gushing upward. In their anger they called upon the negligent guardian, but he, seeing the harm that had come of his forgetfulness, had fled, though it is said he did not escape the angry waters, for they overtook him and drowned him miserably.

A frenzied effort was made to cover up the well and stop the unwelcome flow, but it was useless, and the people of old Bala had to escape as best they could to higher ground. When morning broke they looked out to where their homes had been and saw, instead of their fields and houses, a great lake three miles long and a mile wide.

To-day the lake is five miles long; and they say that on clear days, when its surface is absolutely calm, you may see at the bottom, off Llangower, the ruins and chimneys of the old town that was overwhelmed so long ago.

And, as the old couplet tells, they say too that the spirit of Gower's Well is not yet appeased. On stormy days water appears to ooze up through the ground at new Bala, which is built at the lower end of the lake, and some day they believe that too will be swamped and the waters will cover the valley as far down as Llanfor.

Llyn Tegid is the old name for Bala Lake; it means the lake of beauty, and Bala well deserves that title. Its shores are verdant and beautifully wooded, commanding in many places magnificent distant views of the mountains which encircle it only a few miles [51] away. Its waters teem with fish; trout up to fourteen pounds and pike twice as big have been caught there — but the flyfisher must not expect always such giants. There is salmon-fishing to be had in the Treweryn river in September.

In the neighbourhood are places of wonderful beauty. Dolgelly, nestling beneath great Cader Idris, is easily accessible, as also is that charming seaside town of Barmouth. Bwlch-y-Groes, one of the finest mountain passes in the Principality, is only ten miles away, and an easy excursion takes one across another very beautiful pass to Lake Vyrnwy, which gives to Liverpool its splendid water supply, and provides anglers with magnificent baskets of Loch Leven trout.

All around is a paradise for artists and fishermen, and a country rich in mountain streams, wild woods, and wide, far views unbeaten in any part of Wales.

Bala Lake

[52]

THE FURRY DAY SONG

[53]

T he celebration of "Furry Day," on May 8th each year, at Helston, in South Cornwall, is one of the most interesting survivals of an old custom in the whole country. On "Furry Day" the whole town makes holiday. The people go first into the surrounding country to gather flowers and branches, and return about noon, when the Furry dance begins and continues until dusk; the merrymakers, hand in hand, dancing through the streets and in and out of the houses, the doors of which are kept open for the purpose.

The origin of the word "Furry," and of the song and dance, is lost in the ages. Some authorities hold that these celebrations are a survival of the old Roman Floralia, others that it began in celebration of a great victory gained by the Cornish over the Saxons. The words and music, as they have come down to us, show many signs of Elizabethan origin. The music reproduced here is from a very old setting and contains many crude harmonies unfamiliar at the present day.

There is one line of the song, "God bless Aunt Mary Moses," that most people will find incomprehensible. It refers to the Virgin Mary, "Aunt" being among the Cornish a term of great respect; "Moses" being a corruption of the old Cornish word "Mowes," a maid. "Mary Moses" means literally "Mary the Maid."

[54]

THE FURRY-DAY SONG

[55]

Where are those Spaniards,
        That make so great a boast, O?
They shall eat the grey goose feather,
        And we will eat the roast, O.
In every land, O,
The land where'er we go.
        With *Halantow, &c.*

As for Saint George, O,
        Saint George he was a Knight, O!
Of all the Knights in Christendom,
        Saint Georgy is the right, O!
In every land, O,
The land where'er we go
        With *Halantow, &c.*

God bless Aunt Mary Moses,
        And all her powers and might, O,
And send us peace in merry England,
        Both day and night, O,
And send us peace in merry England,
Both now and evermore, O!
        With *Halantow, &c.*

(Listen to MIDI version of the above)
Sheet Music: Page 1, Page 2.

Robin Hood and little John,

They both are gone to fair, O!

And we will go to the merry green wood

To see what they do there, O!

And for to chase, O!

To chase the buck and doe.

With Halantow,

Rumble Ow!

For we were up as soon as any day, O!

And for to fetch the Summer home,

The Summer and the May, O!

For Summer is a-come, O!

And Winter is a-gone, O!

Where are those Spaniards,

That make so great a boast, O?

They shall eat the grey goose feather,

And we will eat the roast, O,

In every land, O,

The land where'er we go.

With *Halantow, &c.*

As for Saint George, O,

Saint George he was a Knight, O!

Of all the Knights in Christendom,

Saint Georgy is the right, O!

In every land, O,

The land where'er we go.

With *Halantow, &c.*

God bless Aunt Mary Moses,

And all her powers and might, O,

And send us peace in merry England,

Both day and night, O,

And send us peace in merry England,

Both now and evermore, O!

With *Halantow, &c.*

THE FURRY-DANCE TUNE

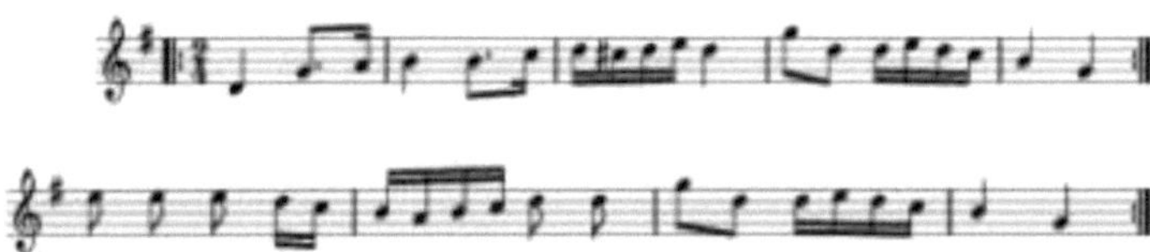

(Listen to MIDI version of the above)
Sheet Music: Page 1.

The simple air only of "The Furry Dance" is given here. It was probably originally played by a musician on the pipe, accompanying himself on the tabor.

[56]

Remote Cornwall is still full of queer old customs and survivals of other days. Helston, the "Metropolis" of that picturesque wild district near the Lizard, forms a perfect setting for this interesting relic of the past, and an ideal centre for those who wish to enjoy the beauties and mystery of one of the most remote corners of our island.

The Furry Dance To-day

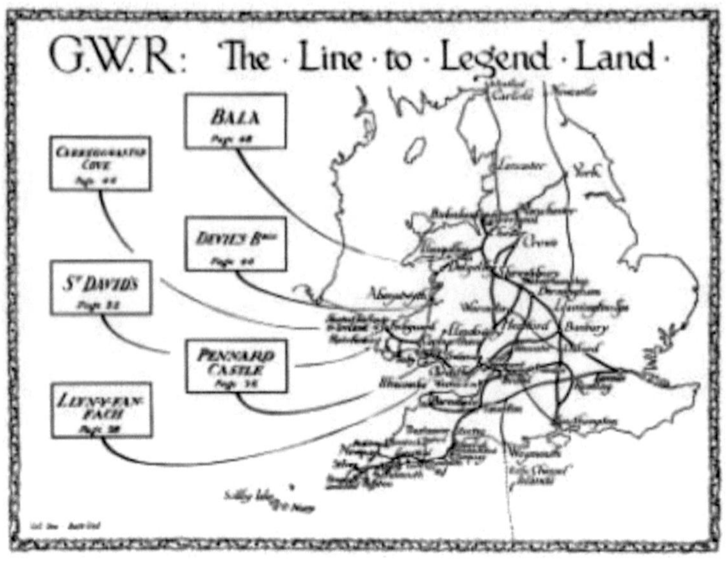

G.W.R: The · Line · to · Legend · Land ·
BALA
CHAPMAN'S COVE
DAVIES BROS
ST DAVIDS
PENNARD CASTLE
LLYN-Y-FAN FACH